I'M ODD,
THANK YOU GOD

CHARLIE
SHEDD

I'M ODD,
THANK YOU GOD

BALCONY PUBLISHING

Salado, TX 76571

Published by: Balcony Publishing, Inc.
            P. O. Box 92, Salado, TX, 76571

Cover design by Dennis Hill
Editors: Ann Nightingale and Mike Plake
"Jesus Laughing" Illustration: Praise Screen Prints

Library of Congress
Catalog Card Number *(Applied For)*
ISBN 0-929488-75-X

10 9   8   7   6   5   4   3   2   1

Printed in the United States of America

To my wife, Anna Ruth, who helps me with my oddities. Isn't it remarkable how Jesus Himself was odd in such wonderful ways! *Lord, help us all to have exactly the oddities that will make us distinctly like you.*

Charlie Shedd

ACKNOWLEDGEMENTS

The author and publisher are deeply grateful to:

Anna Ruth Shedd—who encouraged, inspired, and nudged, always at the right time and in just the right way.

Ann Nightingale—for the initial editing of the original manuscript.

Mike Plake—for the final editing and interior design.

Dennis Hill—for the superb jacket art which appears on this book.

Dr. Gary Moon—for his steadfast and resourceful encouragement in the writing of *I'm Odd, Thank You God.*

Karen (Shedd) Guarino and Peter Shedd—for the numerous ways in which their support nourished the development and publication of this work.

ALSO BY CHARLIE SHEDD

How to Make People Really Feel Loved

Brush of an Angel's Wing

What Children Tell Me About Angels

Letters to My Grandchildren

CONTENTS

CONTENTS

CONTENTS

CONTENTS

PART I

The ODD Idea

✦ 1 ✦

AN ODD BEGINNING

We are at a gorgeous Marriott Hotel in Atlanta. It's an awesome new hotel, forty stories high. And oh what a dining room.

Here we are, and on my right is Heidi, our editor. Plus Gary too, an author and the new young president of a reputable school of psychology.

We have ordered an elegant meal—and here it comes, gourmet at its best. So let's have the blessing. But there stands the waiter, watching us join hands for prayer.

What would you do? You'd do just what we're doing. Well—maybe.

I say, "Would you like to join us for the prayer?"

"Yes, I would," he answers.

But now an unusual happening. As he joins our circle something nudges me to ask, "Would you like to *say* the blessing for us?"

Surprisingly he responds, "Yes, I would." And he prays a beautiful prayer.

Then he's gone.

———✦———

Heidi, to Charlie: "Do you do that often?"

"No."

"Have you ever done it before?"

"No."

"Well, it certainly was odd, Charlie. Very odd."

Now turning to Gary, "You're the president of a school of psychology. Any chance you can help our Charlie?"

After a hearty laugh, Gary says: "Help? Of course we like to think we can help anyone. But isn't it all right to be odd, Heidi? Jesus was certainly odd, wasn't he?" Then showing his familiar smile, he says, "That's enough theology. Let's eat."

So with great gusto we eat and then are off to bed. Yet somehow a clear voice in my heart keeps whispering, *Yes. It's **very** all right to be odd for God.*

The end of our young waiter's story?

Oh no. The next morning when we go for breakfast, here he comes. Big tray in hand for some other customers, but as he moves toward us he stops.

"Sir," he says, "I want to thank you for asking me to pray last night. When I got home, I told my wife what happened, and we both cried. You see, we've strayed away from the Lord. A long way.

"So right there we made a vow. We promised God that next Sunday we'll take our two little boys to Sunday School. And we've decided we're going back to church ourselves. Thank you! Thank you!

Thank you!"

Then before any of us could dry our tears, the waiter was gone. And that was the day *I'm Odd, Thank You God* was born. Thank you, Lord, for these words from your book:

*It is given unto us to know
the mysteries of the Kingdom of God.*
(Matthew 13:11)

❈ 2 ❈

ACTUALLY, THIS BOOK IS QUITE ODD

It's odd that I'm writing this book. Because, you see, I'm 87 years old:

My computer is old.

My hand is unsteady.

My memory gives me problems.

But I still have some ideas I think you'll enjoy.

It's odd that a publisher is publishing this book. How long since you've heard of a publisher putting out a book written by an octogenarian? The last one is probably one of the books of the Bible.

And it's odd that you are reading this book. Because normally in today's culture, people want to read what the younger authors are writing.

So this book is odd; I'm odd for writing it; the publisher is odd for printing it; and, just maybe, you're odd for reading it. Perhaps this is sort of what the Lord meant when he said to the children of Israel,

> *...ye shall be a **peculiar** treasure*
> *unto me.*
> (Exodus 19:5)

❈ 3 ❈
DEFINING *ODD*

Before we go further, it seems important that we ponder this word "odd".

Generally, being odd is considered to be negative. But, to the contrary, if you go to my dictionary you'll find this definition: "Odd carries the meaning: 'extra-ordinary' or 'rare'." It also defines odd as "markedly different from the usual."

We do know, don't we, that Jesus was markedly different from the religious people of his time. But what does that mean for us in our day? Turn now to the Bible and here is our answer:

Let this mind be in you
which was also in Christ Jesus.
(Philippians 2:5)

❧ PART II ❧

LET THIS MIND BE IN YOU

EXTRA ORDINARY STORIES TO NOURISH THE *MIND OF CHRIST* IN YOU

4

AM I MEETING WITH THE LORD OFTEN ENOUGH?

This is a beautiful story from long ago, and I know you'll love it.

Fernando De'Alongo came from a line of Iberian shepherds extending back twenty generations. His ancestors handed this tradition down to him:

Holy Land sheep exceed in the herding instinct. Every morning each sheep takes its place in the grazing line. And it keeps that particular place throughout the day.

Once, however, during the day each sheep leaves its place and goes to the shepherd. Whereupon the shepherd stretches out his hand. Then, here comes the sheep with expectant eyes and mild little baas. When it arrives, the shepherd affectionately whispers a special blessing into the sheep's ears. Next the sheep rubs its master. Rubs him here, rubs him there. After a few minutes of this ritual the same process is repeated.

Then, with apparent gladness

from both, the sheep returns to its feed-
ing line.

Now why would we begin with such a simple story as this? A lamb and its shepherd are not exactly top news.

Or are they? What better way to learn the mind of the Savior!

Didn't Jesus himself say, "Come unto me...and I will give you rest."

And did you know there is an older version of this scripture, which is translated:

Stay with me and
I will give you gladness.
(Matthew 11:28)

⊰ 5 ⊱

AM I LEARNING (MORE AND MORE) THE IMPORTANCE OF PRAYER?

Now for an odd, odd story with a beautiful memory. It happened when I was heading for a funeral. Yes, I was driving at night. Why? Because I had agreed to "fill in" for my special friend, David. He had been called away to his home because his mother was near death.

"Please, Charlie, can you come and take my place at a funeral service?"

Who is David? He's pastor of a large church, and this is his plea. "Do you think you could drive to Iowa and preach for me tomorrow? Please, Charlie! You have your own assistant on your staff, don't you? Please. I need you very, very much. I really need you."

Quickly I said, "Yes, I'll be there, David. You know I have an excellent assistant. And sure, it's a long way from Indiana to Iowa. But friends like us? Of course, I'll be there."

So here I am on the road. Heavy traffic, yes, but, "Thank you Lord", our night is super beautiful! And it's midnight now and I'm hungry. Oh, hurrah, I see a billboard praising the attractive restaurant up ahead. Once more: "Thank you, Lord. How great Thou art!"

But, oh no! When I arrive, there is a sign on the door, "AFTER MIDNIGHT WE SERVE TRUCKERS ONLY".

Who hath disappointment? Me!

But, oh do I love these *unusual* happenings! Just as I am about to leave, here comes a jolly looking young truck driver.

"Hi, Pop," he calls to me, as he closes the door of his gigantic truck. And now he puts out his hand, "Name's Butch. What's yours?" Of course, I give him my name. I point to the sign and explain my hunger. "Oh that's no problem, Pop. They always let us drivers in with our friends and relatives. Come on, we'll be friends and sit together at the counter." So off we go.

Good food? Yes, extra good, plus what a remarkable newfound chum! Quite naturally, he asks, "What are you doing out here so late tonight, Pop? What's your line?"

"My line is preaching, Butch, and I'm going to a church in Iowa for a funeral."

"I go to church, too, Pop. Whenever I can."

Oh, what a night! If I hadn't been there I wouldn't believe what I am about to say. Yet, it did happen exactly as I tell you.

When I told my new friend that I was on my way to preach in Iowa, what do you suppose? Up from his counter seat he jumped and shouted to the other truck drivers: "Hey, you guys. We got a preacher here. This is Sunday, so we should stand up and bow our heads. The Reverend is going to pray for us right now."

I wish you could have seen how the men reacted. Every one of them stood up reverently. All twelve of them, hands folded, heads down.

So I prayed. Then one by one, the truckers came to thank me. And some of them even asked for special prayers. Then we all went back to dinner.

What an evening. What an event. Odd, yes very odd. But you can believe that night was one very holy moment for me.

Thank you Lord! How great Thou art!

And isn't this a credo for us all:

Anytime, any day, anywhere,
we can talk to you, Lord.

6

AM I ABLE TO ACCEPT
THE THINGS I CANNOT CHANGE?

The Junior High Class had been assigned their last English essay. The subject was, "Describe some person you know who represents true greatness." The winner's essay:

"There was a woman who had done a big washing and hung it out on the line. The line broke and her clean clothes fell in the mud. She didn't say a word. She didn't get mad. She just did it over again, and spread it on the grass so it wouldn't fall. But that night, a dog with dirty feet ran over it. Next morning, when she saw it, she didn't fuss or scold or even cry. All she said was: 'Ain't it queer, that old dog didn't miss nothin.' That is what I call true greatness."

How many times this oft' told story has blessed me when I've needed to accept something I couldn't change. I call it the "Gethsemane Principle." Remember? When facing the cross in the Garden of Gethsemane, Jesus prayed:

My Father, if it is possible, may this cup be taken from me. Yet not as I will, but as you will.
(Matthew 26:39)

⟡ 7 ⟡

AM I DOING THE BEST I CAN,
EVEN WHEN I'M HURTING?

They lived in the country and grew some of the best edibles ever raised. Potatoes and corn; and oh those juicy-ripe tomatoes; plus numerous other edibles. Apples, peaches, grapes and watermelons. No wonder countless customers came from near and far to enjoy their produce.

Truly, these were super suppliers of marvelous fresh vegetables and fruit. But that's not all. This farmer and his family were everybody's favorite kind of people. Smiling, laughing, serving, caring.

Then, as if from nowhere, Roger, the father, became seriously ill. He was the head man of this enterprise, and the father of three sons. And each of his boys had a very special wife. They were all winners, and all determined to help their father in every possible way.

So Roger was hospitalized with an unknown illness. Day after day, week after week, he held on as the doctors worked to diagnose his difficulty. They called in the best specialists, and his family called on the Lord over and over.

And how odd it sounded when one day Roger described his new business plan to the family.

"Most of our customers are honest. So we'll

put our produce out in the yard, and we'll cut a money-slot in our front door for buyers to leave their money. With folks like our customers, it's sure to be a winner."

And it was exactly like Roger and his sons knew it would be. Almost no one stole from them; and they prospered. Yes, this went on for three wonderful years.

Then suddenly Roger began an amazing recovery. So much a come-back that soon his doctors let him go home. A few days at first, and then more and more. And I do wish you could have seen him at his window smiling.

He had done his best, even when he was hurting. So say it again:

Trust in the Lord with all thine heart;
and lean not to thine own understanding.
In all thy ways acknowledge Him,
and He shall direct thy paths.
(Proverbs 3:5-6)

⚔ 8 ⚔

AM I GIVING
WHAT I SHOULD BE GIVING?

The story you are about to read is true. It's about Clarence and Agnes. I wish you could have known them. Clarence was a foreman at the machinery mill, and Agnes worked at the garment mill. They had three beautiful children, and everyone at work and at our church loved all of them. Why? Because they represented pure goodness. And when you read their story, you'll say, "Ah, yes!"

Clarence was a plain ordinary soldier boy in the World War. He went to battle with hundreds of others who never came home. But he did come home, and he told it this way:

"We were in one of those awful battles where almost everyone was killed. I happened to survive because five of us had hidden in a deep trench. But it turned out it wasn't deep enough—because all four of my buddies died. It was hardly imaginable to be there and to have lived through a hell like that.

"I was all alone in an old forsaken battle hole, far out from headquarters. I had no one to mend my wounds. And no one to care. Of course I knew Agnes would be waiting for me, but would we ever meet again? Thank God, I could crawl a bit. So even with my wounded legs, I made my way down the trench to my dead buddies. And I found their leftover food.

"Then came the miracle of miracles. The war was nearly at its end. I knew those old long forsaken battlefields would be searched for the dying. I prayed, 'Oh Lord, please let them find me.'

"And they did.

"Then month after month, I lay in the Army hospital praying again and again, 'Thank you! Thank you! But oh Lord, Why me? Why me?'

"I did recover completely in the Army hospital. And when the months had made me well, I went home to marry Agnes."

———————————

But the story didn't stop there.

I was their pastor, and so glad to have them in our church. He was a foreman at the John Deere tractor factory. No big salary, but, yes, a good living. This was during one of those awful depression years. So Agnes worked at the mill as much as she could. With three fine children, you can imagine what it was like with so little to spend. But Clarence and Agnes did manage for themselves and their little ones. And they also managed for others in need. During those years, these two heroic souls did something very unusual. Actually very odd.

Every month they saved enough to buy an overcoat. Why overcoats? Because so many caring fathers came to work with not enough warm protection for themselves.

So during the years of that awful depression, Clarence and Agnes kept this odd practice going. Gifts of twelve overcoats each year for men at the factory. Yes, twelve chilly men who had been using what little they had to care for their children's warmth. But, thanks to Clarence and Agnes, those children's fathers could be warm too.

Now wouldn't you agree that Clarence and Agnes were truly *extraordinary, rare* and *markedly different from the usual?*

There's that question again—am I giving what I should be giving? Remember this:

> *Whoever sows sparingly*
> *will also reap sparingly,*
> *and whoever sows generously*
> *will also reap generously*
> *...for God loves a cheerful giver.*
> (2 Corinthians 9:6-7)

❧ PART III ❧

Childhood
Learning To Be Extra Ordinary

❧ 9 ❧

MY FATHER WAS A WOODWORKER
"PAR EXCELLENCE"

When I was four years old, my father some-times let me "work" with him in his woodshop. Actually it wasn't much more than a junk room. But yes, he did wonders in it. He was a genius at making old wood into beautiful furniture pieces. And that's when I began learning from him how to turn the *old* into the *new*. Plus saws, hammers, nails, and knives—these became some of my earli-est childhood friends.

Up and down the alleys we'd go, looking for wood scraps. Those were days of little money, and there we were, gladly finding and collecting other people's "throwaways".

Did I love all this? And did I hate all this? Of course! My major problem was right across the street from where we worked. Yes, friends were playing in the ball field where they could wave to me while I was working—and they were having fun.

But it was a time of my gradually learning to shut up, put up, and look up.

Interesting, isn't it, how some things we thought were negatives turn out beautifully posi-tive. Through all the years of my adult life, making new furniture with old discarded boards has been one of my most extraordinary pleasures.

Some days I can hear the Lord himself say: "You can thank your father for all that woodwork training in turning old things into new."

And isn't this what the Lord was talking about when he made his ODDEST proclamation ever:

> *...Verily, verily, I say unto thee,*
> *except a man be born again,*
> *he cannot see*
> *the kingdom of God.*
> (John 3:3b)

❧ 10 ☙

MY MOTHER WAS A SUPER TEACHER

My mother was a super teacher, but in my childhood days I often did not agree with her.

Both of my parents were much older than most mothers and fathers of other children my age, so I guess that's why she expected more from me.

When I was only four, Mother took me to her Ladies Aid meetings. And she would have me get up before the group to do various forms of entertainment. Such as bible verses, stories, and jokes.

Having been a teacher of young drama students, she trained me with such gems as: "Eyes up. Eyes down. Smile now. Now frown."

Oh yes, and at first she even thought I might be a singer. So she taught me hymns, both old and new favorites. But, thank Heaven, her attempt to make me a singer took care of itself. The Ladies Aid grudgingly agreed that singing was not my specialty.

So, with that settled, I became "The Little Boy Public Speaker." Bible stories, general stories, and occasional humor. Those latter items I loved. And I still do. So, though I long harbored resentments toward my mother for her demanding ways, she virtually led me through a pre-school "seminary" that developed my lifelong ministry skills.

The Good Book assures us that when we get to heaven, all past, present, and future will turn to positive joys. But if you have been carrying any negatives about anyone, even your parents, you don't have to wait for heaven to get relief. Here's a simple little prayer I know will give you courage to find the positive joys in your life:

Dear Lord, before I get to heaven help me to put away any and all negatives I ever carried for anyone. And may I begin today searching 'The Book of Books' for this verse:

...and forgive our trespasses,
as we forgive those who trespass against us.
(Matthew 6:12)

❧ 11 ❧

MISS FANCHON'S "NEVER EVER" LIST

If you had known her, I'm sure you would never forget Miss Fanchon. And I'm certain too you'll get what she called "a plain vanilla bit of wisdom." She also labeled it, "The Seven Never Evers to Never Forget."

Whatever your age, you should never ever treat these "Seven Never Evers" lightly.

1. NEVER EVER LIE

2. NEVER EVER HATE

3. NEVER EVER CHEAT

4. NEVER EVER SCORN

5. NEVER EVER FORGET TO BE THANKFUL

6. NEVER EVER BREAK THE TEN COMMANDMENTS

7. NEVER EVER FAIL TO PRAY EACH DAY, AND OFTEN

It sounds so simple, doesn't it? That was one reason I loved Miss Fanchon. She had an amazing ability to keep life simple—as a teacher, a neighbor, a true friend, and "another mother" to me.

From the time I was five years old to the third grade, she was my mentor. No wonder when we moved away I longed to stay with her forever. But when that didn't happen, she stayed right with me in my heart. And now at eighty-seven, I'm still praising the Lord for Miss Fanchon.

I recommend you learn and live by her "Never Ever" list. Oh yes, I know, that would be somewhat odd; but if you do, someday you'll thank God you did.

MISS FANCHON'S EIGHTH
"NEVER EVER" PRINCIPLE

Watching our second graders play baseball might be more fun than you'd imagine. But one person out there on the ball field was not having a good time. The problem was that little Ronnie could only stand and watch. His legs were seriously crippled; so much so that he would never be able to play baseball. Yet game after game he came to the ball field. He stood there watching his friends and longing to be a normal boy.

Miss Fanchon was one of those very special teachers. One of her enthusiastic mottos was: "I am here to bless everyone of you."

She and I lived on the same block and we were extra special buddies. Yes, we really were very much in love. But I was five and she was nearing sixty, the age teachers were forced to retire. (All the students and teachers thought this was ridiculous, that she had to retire at 60! Ridiculous. Oh yes.)

But back to Ronnie.

Miss Fanchon came up with incredible ideas when they where needed. For instance, she said, "Why not let Ronnie *umpire* your baseball games? I think that would be good for all of you students and for him."

The result? We made him our umpire. And everyone loved him. And Miss Fanchon's idea.

Now can you believe that another amazing fact followed?

Ronnie went right up the ladder: umpiring from grade to grade. Even in high school and on into his collegiate education years. All the way, he umpired.

You can see it, can't you? A crippled boy becoming a huge success, plus being everyone's favorite at the same time.

Thank you, Miss Fanchon, for teaching us all your wonderful mottos. Such as the eighth one: "NEVER EVER GIVE UP ON ANYONE."

And how very odd! It's that same truth again, right out of the Good Book:

> *Whoever sows sparingly*
> *will also reap sparingly,*
> *and whoever sows generously*
> *will also reap generously.*
> (2nd Corinthians 9:6)

❧ 13 ❧

MY UNCLE EDGER'S SUMMER JOB

My Uncle Edger was School Superintendent in a small Iowa town. He had been one of those college professors all the students loved. He was highly intelligent, fun, and everybody's favorite teacher. But then came the days of the Great Depression. It was an awful affliction upon everyone, especially teachers.

So, why did my uncle move to this small town? Because in his new position he'd have a much better income. My aunt (his wife) was also a teacher in the same little school, and she also earned an adequate salary.

They had two daughters ready for college. No wonder he took his new position. This little town was one of the few prosperity centers anywhere. You ask how could that be? Well, there was only one factory here, but it did pay well. And why? Because the flourishing little factory manufactured necessities for the public.

That's why everyone urged my Uncle Edger to make such a change to this little Iowa town.

And during the summer he also had another chance to earn extra money. He, being a former farm boy, could drive a horse team during threshing season. And that he did.

So Uncle Edger worked during the summer. His job was what they called, a "Hurry-up Wagon Driver." And he was also very efficient, so they were always glad to have him. Besides, he was extra wise.

It was truly an exciting time during "threshing" season. Cut the crop, pile it in the big horse wagon, and go, go, go. Take it to the mill, have it weighed, and shovel it into the grain lifts. Then hurry back to the threshing machines as fast as you can. Why the rush? Because the wagons that made the most "runs" would earn the most dollars.

I can still see those beautiful Belgian horses they gave him to drive. Small wonder he was so proud of pulling his wagons of grain to its storing place. You do remember those great skyscraper silo centers, don't you? They were so dramatic, towering up from the flat farm land. And such highly valuable facilities for storing the grain until it was ready for shipping.

The first year I worked with my Uncle Edger I was twelve years old. What a thrill! Riding along and helping him in little things. Getting to hold the horses' reins now and then, and listening to his wisdom. It was any boy's ideal summer adventure.

But it turned out that this was one of those "rain, rain, rain" seasons. So, as usual, my practical Uncle Edger would use his "extra wise" brain and share it with me. One rainy day he said,

"Charlie, this is one of those times when you slow down to get ahead. You see how I do it? I turn the horses into a safe rut, which has dried up a bit. See those other wagons are going fast, hoping to arrive first. But you get it, don't you? Lots of them will find their loads sinking down in the mire, and they'll get stuck. So this is the message, Charlie: *Sometimes you have to slow down to get ahead.*"

Yes, that's what he said. And if you put on your thinking cap one more time, you might want to add this other little gem he taught me:

...but remember, Charlie,
being in a rut
usually is good only temporarily.

❈ PART IV ❈

HIGH SCHOOL, COLLEGE, SEMINARY

STILL LEARNING
TO BE EXTRA ORDINARY

14

SOMETIMES YOU MUST GET OUT
TO GET IN

I thought I was number one, and I wanted everybody to know it. Well, why not? Here I was, just a freshman, and playing first string football. Yes, I had forgotten it was only because of my size.

Of course all this seemed outstanding to a country boy like me. And no one up to now had called my attention to the good qualities of humility. So alas, I had made a fool of myself with the team; with my classmates; at home; and everywhere.

So one morning Dr. Smiley (our school superintendent) called me in for a conference.

"Sit down Smartie!" he began. "I mean right over there in the corner. Yes, sit there where you can't possibly get away from me.

"You're not going to like this, but your time has come. You are absolutely unbearable. The teachers and too many students are turning thoroughly negative toward you.

"I want you to go to your locker. Get everything out of it and scat! I mean you're not welcome here anymore. You are destroying the original Charlie."

He went on, "This is my advice. Go home

and visit those beautiful woods behind your house. The first day, lie down under the trees and ask yourself, 'Did I create these trees and the wild flowers here? Or did the Lord Himself create them?' Stay there all day and think, think, think.

"Then the next day go down to the river and take a long walk on the shore. And as you watch the water flowing, this time ask yourself, 'What part did I have in making nature so beautiful?'

"Finally, for a farewell, when you're done with the first two days, you come back here and give me a report."

So now, was I listening to what he was saying? You better believe it!

"You must learn something all important. Yes, Charlie, something for you to never forget. When you think you're so ultra self-made, you've lost it. God is the Lord of life, not you. And when you can confess that, when you can put aside your self-image as 'number one', you'll be healthy again. Then we'll welcome you back."

All these thoughts came pouring out of my superintendent. Plus thoughts even more pensive came from the Lord Himself. They came to me over the next two days as I lay among those beautiful trees. And also as I walked beside God's beautiful river.

I found there was only one solution. So I said to myself: "Charlie, you must go back to school, confess your foolishness, and ask forgiveness."

So that's what I did.

And as I walked back to school I prayed: "Oh Lord, now I see the truth. Thank you for making this clear to me. Thank you for my wise school superintendent too. From now on I will live by this bible verse a Sunday school teacher once taught me: *Create in me a clean heart O God, and renew a right spirit within me.* (Psalm 51:10).

For a high school freshman, that was some kind of major readjustment. And I prayed,

Dear Lord, keep me
forever readjusting to your way.

🔳 15 🔳

COLLEGE FOOTBALL

We were all sure of an extra good team that year. And every one of us in uniform hoped for a first team position. Which position meant we'd be eligible for board and room. How much did that matter? It mattered much, because those were Great Depression years.

So there we were, out for first day practice. There were forty of us sitting down on the football field, waiting for our head coach. And there he came, a well-known "championship winning" leader.

After a brief greeting, he began describing what he expected of us. Such as, "I want you guys to understand: I'm tough! Yes sir, very tough." A statement he followed with vulgar swearing.

Then the oddest thing happened? One of the guys spoke up. And this someone was a tackle whose real name was Harry; but we called him "Monsignor".

Up he jumped and shouted, "You are not for me coach! I could never put up with your language. Goodbye."

He tossed his helmet at the coach's feet, and headed for the dressing room. Then suddenly he turned around to us, and big Harry said, "Any of you guys wanna come with me?"

"Yes." Eight of us went with him back to the gym. And there we sat on the dressing room benches utterly stunned—more at what we had done than at what the coach had said.

No one said anything? There was only stony silence. And then, after what seemed like a decade, Monsignor spoke.

"Well guys, I guess I owe you all an apology. You know this means no school for us this year. Our chance for scholarships this late would be zero anywhere."

Then, at that very moment, the coach came into the gym. Apologize? Oh yes. With a begging address he finished something like this: "Honest guys, I didn't mean to offend you. The truth is I get over enthused with a high-potential squad like you. I must admit I'm noted for being tough. And this is the first time in twenty years I've had such an objection. But please listen to me. We've just got to have you on the team. With men like you, I know we can win the league and be the best ever."

He hesitated and said again, "Please accept my apology and come on back. I promise you I'll try not to offend you again."

With no further pleading he was gone.

Now once more it was big Harry speaking: "What do you say men? We all know he's a top-notch coach. And at least he knows now we won't put up with his language. Don't you think it's possible the Lord would want us out there this year teaching our coach while he teaches us?"

Back out to the field we went. And what a season! Nine games undefeated and our coach honestly trying to clean up his talk. Plus the Monsignor, being a joker, called this "A year of cleaning up, for heaven's sake."

Whenever we could, years later, we would meet to renew our friendships. And, of course, every time we met Harry reminded us that he did become a monsignor for his beloved Catholic Church.

🔯 16 🔯

THE LITTLE HILL CHURCH

Uphill, downhill, horses and cattle along the way. And always a warm greeting. "Meet you in church, Charlie." It was a wonderful two year memory that changed my life forever. Here's how it happened.

Emery played right beside me on our college football team. You can understand what happened with the two of us, shoulder to shoulder, winning game after game.

So what else could I do when he said, "Come on, Charlie. Meet me Sunday at our Little Hill Church. It's just up the road from my home. I know you'll love it."

And he was so right. I did love it—after a while, that is.

What I didn't know was that the Little Hill preacher had told them "goodbye" just last Sunday.

So here we are; it's Sunday morning and a complete surprise. As I approach the Little Hill Church, here comes Emery with his friends.

"Charlie boy, our preacher left us last Sunday and we want you to be our preacher today. You speak a lot at the college, and you always have something to say around campus. So today it's *you* at the Little Hill Church."

Once again, what can I do? Here's my bosom buddy and football teammate, and I'm without excuses for denying the plea of such a friend.

"Charlie, these people like jokes *and* football, so come on now."

I did just what he said, and kept on doing it for two solid years. (Yes, before my seminary days in Chicago).

It was every Sunday in the Little Hill Church (except when we were playing the fall season games out of town). Of all my churches, this one is a memory supreme. And oh boy, what I learned about preaching.

And then there were those wonderful dinners the Little Hill Church members served their young preacher. Especially Mr. and Mrs. Wilson. They were an elderly couple who lived on their beautiful farm where they had retired. But their guidance and loving spirit never retired.

I will say though that Mr. Wilson sometimes got his sense of humor and theology tangled up a bit.

Like one Sunday when I was enjoying dinner at their house, and Mr. Wilson said: "Preacher Boy, have you ever noticed that after church, when you come down our lane to eat with us, this always happens. Our chickens run right over there and put their necks down on the chopping block. You watch, you'll see. Those are 'thinking' chickens my wife raised. Just listen and you can almost hear them saying: 'Let me be the next chicken to give my life for the preacher.' And doesn't our bible say we'll all go to heaven if we give ourselves to the Lord?"

Now that's some kind of theology isn't it? Well, maybe a bit *too* odd.

◈ 17 ◈

LOVE THAT MR. WRIGLEY

During my seminary years, I started out on my admiration for Mr. Wrigley, and for his professional baseball team, the Chicago Cubs.

In our very first year at seminary, they were headed for the top. And, oh glory, they played only a few miles away from our campus. It so happened that we didn't understand the afternoon "hermaneutics" classes any more than our instructors. But oh my, oh my, we would sure understand a World Series baseball championship.

Unfortunately, ticket prices to the games were considerably more than poor seminary students could manage on a frequent basis.

One Sunday morning at church (during the sermon) up came a brilliant idea. Our big Presbyterian congregation downtown was both our choice and Mr. Wrigley's. Our idea was to write a letter to him asking for reduced ticket prices. I wrote:

"Dear Mr. Wrigley,

"We are writing this letter addressed to you and your baseball Cubs. Knowing that you are a friend of our seminary, we have a special request. Could you give us a ticket price reduction? Our ministerial students are super rooters for you to win the World Series this year. You also know that ministerial students would be short of money.

"If that is possible, we can assure you we will make strong supporters of your Cubs..."

He wrote us back saying:

"This very week our team is playing at home and we welcome you. Go to Gate Five for tickets that we have reduced in price for you."

And what do you suppose we found out when we went to Gate Five? Mr. Wrigley had left a note that read: *For today's game and all games this season, McCormick Seminary students will always come in free!*

Hurrah! Doesn't our bible say: "GOD MOVES IN A MYSTERIOUS WAY HIS WONDERS TO PERFORM."

Some may think this serious verse definitely does not apply to baseball games for seminary students. I'm just ODD enough to believe that it definitely DOES!

◼ PART V ◼

ON-THE-JOB LEARNING
TO BE MARKEDLY DIFFERENT

18

TOO MUCH DRINKING
AT THE WEDDING

It happened at a fashionable mid-western church. I was the new minister, just called to their pulpit. I was also a very young man who was brought to this large church for what they called my "unusual ability". Some labeled me, "Smile, Laugh and Let 'em Have it Son". (Quite some label, wasn't it?) But they did pack the church almost every Sunday for their "Preacher Boy". Chairs in the aisles sometimes, too.

It was "Rehearsal Night" now for the wedding of a favorite daughter. Her father is the top executive in one of the city's major factories. And here they are for the gala "Pre-Wedding Celebration."

Fun. Fun. An exciting occasion for sure, except for one thing. Most of the folks have been pre-celebrating at their country club by drinking too much. So? So, what it means is that the rehearsal is a near disaster.

Then suddenly comes the firm voice of their "Preacher Boy". "Hear me now," I call out, and they listen. "I want all of you to take a seat. I also want one hundred percent attention. Why? Because, except for a few of you, there has been far too much drinking for a wedding rehearsal. As your pastor, I remind you that marriage is a sacrament, dedicated to the Lord. But you're making it a desecration. There's no more rehearsal tonight. It's over.

"Instead, you go straight home and sober up. Understand my warning. Tomorrow night if any of you have been drinking before the wedding, *there will be no wedding*. And believe me, I myself will check each of you personally."

———

Oh the silence—a very cold silence, as one by one they left the church.

You know what happened? What happened was that at the wedding the next day the entire congregation was sober, in toto. Which was quite odd for this church!

And to the glory of God, everyone said: "This was the most beautiful wedding ever in our church."

But that's not all. Early Monday morning my office bell rang. It was my secretary calling to say, "The bride's father is here. He wants to see you."

Very sternly, the father placed his coat over the back of one of my office chairs, and then made this speech: "Preacher Boy, as you know, I was on the committee that brought you to be our minister. And last Friday night you sent all of our wedding participants home early for excessive drinking, including me." He dropped his eyes and stared at the carpet. "And you made me so angry! Very angry! And my wife was furious!

"But I have come here this morning to say, 'Thank you'. Fact is, a hearty 'Thank you'. This church has long needed a minister like you. I see that now. We've really needed you! So I come to tell you this: From now on, if there is ever anything I can do for you, you be sure to let me know. Thank you, Son. God bless you as He has blessed us in our perfectly beautiful wedding."

Oh yes, and can't you just imagine there was a special celebration in heaven. I'm sure of this as well—the Lord beamed one of His broadest smiles.

19

THE FARMER AND THE PREACHER

Bruce was a fine young farmer in Minnesota. His hobby was breeding champion Collie dogs. I was a minister in Oklahoma, and I too raised quality Collies. We became close friends by correspondence. As we learned to appreciate each other's dogs, we learned to appreciate each other.

Then in one of his letters, Bruce surprised me with this confession: "What a deep satisfaction it must give you to be a parish pastor. My father is an Episcopal priest, and I have a confession to make. So many times I wish I'd followed in his footsteps. Tell me, Charlie. Is the ministry as satisfying to you as it looks to me from here?"

What an absolutely fascinating coincidence. That very week I had written Bruce a letter almost identical to his: "Tell me, is farming as satisfying to you as it looks to me?"

You remember those two letters, don't you Bruce? And of course we both remember the outcome. You voted for farming because you simply couldn't give it up. And thank you Bruce, for your letter to me. I wouldn't have changed places either. Not for anything.

Rejoice in the Lord always, and again I say, Rejoice.
(Phillipians 4:4)

20

MY GOD AND I

Did you ever say or write something so unusual that you could only say, "These words came *through* me, not *from* me." This is what happened to me with the song, "My God and I."

There is a well-known Latvian hymn by Sergie which begins, "My God and I go in the fields together; we walk and talk as good friends should and do." When properly sung, "My God and I" is one of the most beautiful of our ecclesiastical anthems.

One Sunday morning when I was pastor of my first church an amazing thing happened. I was trying my best to recover the words of the Latvian song for my congregation. We had the music, but not the words.

From the back door of our church in La Salle, Colorado, we had a magnificent view of Long's Peak and Mount Meeker. As I stood looking at the sun rise on those majestic peaks, I prayed that I might remember the words for Sergie's hymn.

Then suddenly, here came "My God and I" as printed below. No, these were not Sergie's words. Nor were they "mine" in the purest sense. *They had come through me, but not from me.* I am not musically gifted. I am a lover of music, yet not a composer of music.

And here is an astonishing bit of information. Even I am awed by a bookseller's report: "In our store, Charlie, your version almost always sells more than the original." Believe me, I'm not in any way downgrading Sergie. As I said, he was a musician and I am not. But that day I was only a young minister who needed Divine help.

An "odd" happening, wasn't it? Yes, very odd. But here are the lyrics that came *through* me.

MY GOD AND I: A Hymn

My God and I,
We walk the hills together.
My God and I,
We walk so tenderly.
We climb the mounts
Of sorrow, pain, and trouble.
My God and I,
We walk unendingly.

We do not know
The joy that comes with riches.
We do not care
That pleasure comes with fame.
We only know
We walk life's trails together.
My God and I,
Still will we walk the same.

And though I've sinned,
He knows each fallen moment.
And though I've erred,
He cares enough for me
To wash me clean
Of every stain and evil.
My God and I,
We walk forgivingly.

My God and I,
We walk the hills together.
My God and I,
We walk so tenderly.
We climb the mounts
Of sorrow, pain, and trouble.
My God and I,
We walk unendingly.

(Given straight from the choirs of heaven to a young preacher.)

※ 21 ※

NORMAN AND THE ANGELS

Do you have certain friends to whom you'd wholeheartedly say, "I thank the Lord you're still on earth with me. It's so good to know you're reachable if I need you."

Norman and I are like that. We grew up together in our little Iowa town. We went to school together, played together, and loved our beautiful river together. Sometimes we'd sleep all night at the river: fishing, cooking, talking, laughing, loving our river.

After eighty years, we're still buddies. Almost never together these days, except by phone. But oh those memories.

Some years ago, the time had come for our high school class to celebrate its sixtieth reunion. Whenever possible, Martha and I had been there every fifth year, and it was wonderful. Except it was never quite right for me because Norman couldn't make it. His wife was ill for many years. She was bedridden and he couldn't permit himself to leave her. Why not? Because, thank God, some couples are odd like that. In time, her doctors said she was permanently unconscious; but still Norman walked two miles to the hospital, every day, to "visit" her.

"It's all so sad, Charlie." He poured out his

heart to me. "She doesn't know me. But I keep hoping she understands *something*. I hum for her, read a little from her bible, say a prayer. It's hard. But think how difficult it must be for her if she's even a little bit conscious. There are times I tell the Lord, 'Please take her home. She'd be so much happier with You.'

"Oh, and I forgot to tell you one thing. Once in a while she squeezes my hand, and that gives me a little hope. So with all this you can see why I could never come to the reunions. No way that could be right."

No way? I thought to myself. Norman are you sure? The bible says over and over, "The Lord has ways we know not of." How about angels? So I decided to have a talk with Norman. I could introduce him to angels, couldn't I?

And that's what I did.

———————✦———————

Conversation between two old river buddies:

"Norman, do you believe in angels?"

"Well I read things about 'em sometimes, and I've seen a few angel shows on T.V. But do you really believe all that stuff, Charlie? I mean, about real live angels. You go for that stuff?"

"Yes, I go for that, Norman. Only it isn't 'stuff'.

You need to get away once in a while. And if you pray for her every day while you're gone, I believe one of God's special angels will take your prayer to her bedside—and help her to feel your presence."

"You sure you know what you're talking about Charlie?"

"Well I'd better be sure. I've written two books on angels. Tell you what. You promise to read them and I'll send you an autographed copy of each book. No charge."

"Wow, that's some offer! But let me sleep on it, Charlie. I'll call you back."

He did call back (before he read my books). And he did come to the reunion. And everybody loved his jokes. That's Norman. But after a few hours he got serious and took me aside: "Now Charlie, you told me if I'd say my prayers for my wife every day one of those angels would come and take my prayers back to her. That still on?"

"Yes sir, it's still on."

"But I have another question, Charlie: Do I say those prayers silently or out loud?"

"Norman, you always did ask questions no one else would ask. But since I've never heard this one before, here's what I'd do. I'd go down to the river, take a walk, and say my prayers out loud." So that's what he did.

Then on the last day of our reunion Norman

said: "Charlie, I got another question. These angels, do they operate out of Los Angeles? You know, I haven't seen my brother, Jim, in years. Didn't I hear you say once they work out of anywhere?"

"Yes, Norman, you heard me."

So he went to Los Angeles, and that too was a beautiful experience. Me? I hurried home to finish another book on angels.

You think we're through. Oh no. The phone rang and you guessed it—Norman again.

"Charlie, I got another question. Those angels you're so high on, do they work out of Ann Arbor, Michigan? You know my daughter. I haven't seen her in a long, long time."

"No problem, Norman, you can count on it. They'll be glad to help you again in Ann Arbor."

"Wow! Some deal, those angels."

"You said it, Norman. Some deal."

Are they (angels) not all ministering spirits,
sent forth to minister for them
who shall be heirs of salvation.
(Hebrews 1:4)

✻ 22 ✻

EIGHTY YEARS PLUS

Dear reader, may you too be able some day to say, "Yes I'm aging and odd. Thank you God."

For eighty-seven years I've had the fun of loving people. Plus the joy of being loved by most of them. If you're not in your eighties yet, keep on loving and you will see.

When you get truly old an interesting thing may happen in your memory. You stand at the foot of your stairs asking, "Was I going downstairs from here or was I going upstairs?" When that happens, say a quickie prayer, "Lord. You'll guide me won't you?" And He will. It's in The Book!

Turn to your bible. It will guide you day or night. Being a believer can be a matter of study when your mind is young or old. Age is not the critical factor, though years can make you wiser.

So say it with me: Any age, anytime, any day, anywhere—the Lord is ready for your friendship.

"...as I was with Moses, so will I be with you. I will not fail you or forsake you."
(Joshua 1:5)

◆ PART VI ◆

ODD EXPERIENCES IN FAMILY LIFE

23

WHEN MARTHA PLAYED SOLOMON

Family devotions was a most interesting time for everyone in our family. Why? We had all designed this ritual together. But one particular night I would never forget.

We began with "Interesting Things." Meaning all seven of us had to share what we called "Interesting Things." This meant the discussion of something interesting, something fun, or something needing serious thought.

But you don't want to participate? That's O.K. If your day was a bore and you don't want to talk. "Just put your quarter over there in the penalty box and listen to the rest of us." How many quarters ever saw that box? Very few.

Five children and two parents do not a boring family make. Fun, laughter, frivolous bits of this and that. But sometimes on the deep side of our emotions there would be some striking surprises.

It was one of those nights. At her turn, our only daughter, Karen, did something different. Instead of the usual report, she asked a question for discussion.

Her question came slowly and with meaning. "Momma. Say all six of us are out in a boat and you are on the shore. But you could only save one of us from drowning. Who would it be?"

All heads turned now to "Momma." What would she say? At last she spoke and what she said was pure Danish. Danish meant you'd think real hard, then you'd say exactly what you thought. You'd say it as lovingly as you could, but you'd say it clearly and without falter. So she did.

"No question. I'd save your father."

Long silence. Five stunned children, one of whom began to cry; two of whom went to their rooms; two others sat like stone monuments.

Awesome, awful, staggering. Was it good or was it bad? Think about it. What possible blessing could anyone receive from a night like this?

What we got was five children who would tell you today: "That was without doubt the most solidifying night of all those years in our entire family devotions. Mom and Dad were a solid duo."

Odd isn't it, how some of our most shattering moments come back one day with a different label? From "I'm not sure I like that," to "Yes, yes, a thousand times yes." Thank you! Thank you, Lord!

❖ 24 ❖

OH THE WISDOM OF A LITTLE CHILD

It was the fall season, time for officer sessions on our church budget. We were meeting in our home. Eleven elders and I, their minister, discussing possibilities.

Then it happened. Little Philip had escaped his bed once more. So there he was, downstairs in his pajamas. Did he want something to eat? Something to discuss? No. Apparently he had something quite different on his mind.

So once more, I gave him the same scolding. "Philip. Can't you see your daddy is busy? How many times have I told you this is a very important church meeting. And didn't I tell you three times we don't need you. Please, for heaven's sake, won't you leave us alone?"

Then came our little boy's answer, and I will never forget it. Never! Crawling up into my lap, he replied, "But Daddy, all I want is to be close to you forever."

And would you believe, one of our officers said, "Preacher Charlie, you do know don't you that the bible says, 'A little child shall lead them'." From that day on, I could never forget that my little son only wanted to be near his father.

Lord help me to want to be close to you forever.

*We are children of God
...heirs with Christ
...that we may be glorified by
Him.*
(From Romans 8: 16-18)

❖ 25 ❖

JARRETT AND GOLIATH

My grandson, Jarrett, and I were sitting again on his parent's glassed in front porch. It was here that he and I had written our book, *What Children Tell Me About Angels*.

So now we were discussing the possibility of another "Grandson-Grandpa" book, and he had just made a fascinating suggestion. "Great idea, Jarrett. You're growing up fast. So lets do a book on some unusual happenings in the Bible. You have some thoughts?"

"Sure," he said. "That's easy. How about David and Goliath? You know what I mean, 'Young Brother Kills Big Brother's Enemy.'"

"Keep going, Jarrett. How would that happen?"

"That's easy too. Compared to Goliath, David was just a mite, but any time you think you're bigger than God, somebody's going to hit you in the head with a rock!!!"

That grandson of mine *is* odd! Thank you God!

❖ 26 ❖

MOLECULES

We have gathered in what she calls her "Beautiful Garden Room." It's in the home of a lovely church woman who delights in entertaining her family, friends, and guests. And everyone who knows her loves the way she does it.

So this is another one of those happy celebrations in her home. Her church has invited me to be their speaker. But before the actual speaking event, this is the Preparation Committee welcoming me as their guest.

Then suddenly, right before my eyes, I see something quite extraordinary. There by the divan stands our beautiful hostess. She's bent over, head down, praying with a woman seated in a chair.

Most unusual. A private prayer time for two in the midst of such a gala event? And fortunately not heard by the other guests are the words that spring into my mind: "Dear Lord, what a beautiful combination of molecules you have fashioned in this lovely lady!"

As I stand there watching, I am deeply touched. In all my years, how many times have I seen such a happening? We'll call this, "heavenly reverence mixed with joy and laughter."

And why would my mind turn to an unusual

word like "molecules"? Interesting how unusual words do sometimes come at unusual times.

Do you know what the word "molecule" means? One of the meanings I found is, "perfection with everything in its place." And why I would be drawn to this word at this time? But why not? My dictionary also says that "molecule" sometimes denotes a "collection of all things needed."

Now that's a perfect label for an extra lovely lady isn't it? Her name is Anna Ruth. And would you believe, she is now my wife, my chosen one, whom I still call, "My Lady of The Extraordinary Molecules." Odd, yes. But she likes it, and so do I.

Nothing could be wrong with that, could it? After all, our bible says:

> *And God saw everything that*
> *He had made, and behold,*
> *it was very good.*
> (Genesis 1:31)

◈ 27 ◈

CHAPEL BY THE LAKE

Anna Ruth and I are on an afternoon drive to our favorite lake. We love the water, the people, their boats, and the fish.

We come to a chapel right on the lake. Almost at the same moment we say, "Don't you just love chapels?" So, we get out to have a look. And isn't this interesting! A beautiful young couple comes out of the chapel.

Their names are Jennifer and John. And they are not here for just a casual look. We find that these two are to be married soon, and this is the place they've selected for the ceremony.

Their situation: "This is our number one choice, *but* we have a problem. The minister we were counting on has moved away."

Anna Ruth looks at me with a smile. Then in her happiest voice she says, "My best friend happens to be a minister. I think he might be just the man for you. He's not only a minister but an author too, and I know you'd love him."

"That's wonderful," they say almost in unison. "Where do we find him?"

"How about right here by my side," she smiles at me, and I laugh. Then all four of us hug, laugh, and are amazed. Amazed at what? Amazed at the way our Lord moves in His mysterious ways. And then tears of sweet gladness come to all our eyes. Of course, the Lord Himself is here.

Then the five of us begin making plans for this Heavenly directed wedding. Set the date and book the three required sessions for engaged and clergy to meet.

So I ask, "Are you sure you want me to be your 'marrying pastor'? We will need to meet several times for serious discussions about your marriage. That's a rule in our denomination. And you live a considerable distance from us."

But it all works out, and the day finally arrives for this beautiful wedding. Parents, grandparents, numerous friends. Oh yes. Young and old alike praise the Lord. Once more. Yes. Oh yes.

A wedding and marriage we'll remember forever. O Lord, our Lord, how great Thou art!

...and the two will become one.
(Ephesians 5:31)

◆ 28 ◆

ANNA RUTH AND CHARLIE
GET MARRIED

It's a beautiful day at Ardmore's Noble Chapel. And we are all ready for a major event. This is the wedding of Anna Ruth and Charlie.

Not one single empty pew and the organ is in its glory. Candles and orchids and angels adding their beauty.

Here comes the bride and, yes, the groom too. "Behold the way of a man with a maid."

He is eighty-four. She a mere eighty. And you can hear the congregation whispering: "Don't you hope they'll live together a good long time."

Now the ceremony is over and the bride steps forward. Smiling to her many friends she says: "May I say a word or two?"

Of course she may and she does. Very nice. "Thank you, dear friends, for sharing this wonderful time with us." And after other accolades and smiles, she turns to her groom and says, "Charlie, will you please say a word, too?"

Of course, he will. He's a preacher, isn't he? Wouldn't any clergyman of experience have profound words for such an event? And this is his profound message:

"Thank you. Thank you. Does anyone here have a question?"

Yes, Charlie Shedd was speechless—the first such occurrence in 84 years. The guests sat in stunned silence for a long three or four seconds. Then suddenly the chapel filled with laughter, a "joyful noise" that, years later, would sustain Anna Ruth and Charlie through many a difficult day.

❖ 29 ❖

ALL THESE ODDITIES IN ONE DAY!

It was a rainy Spring morning. We made our way to the large Oklahoma University Hospital. New to us, and in a downpour, very difficult to find.

At last we did locate the huge building, and there we were at their mammoth underground parking area. But oh woe, not even one open parking place; whatever could we do? Then suddenly, as we neared the main door, there was a car leaving right ahead of us. "Thank you, Lord. How great Thou art!"

We walked into the huge complex. Abruptly, Charlie remembered: "Honey, I can hardly believe this. I left my briefcase in the car. Wouldn't you know it? I planned to do some writing on our book while you are in the doctor's office."

So Anna Ruth reached for her keys. "Oh no. I must have left my keys in the car, too." And back we went. Just as we found our parking place, a young man stopped his car and asked: "Did you folks lose your keys?"

"We certainly did. Please tell us, have you found them?"

"Yes," he replied with one of the most beautiful smiles ever. "Are you aware that people in this

milieu pick up fallen keys and drive away with sto-
len cars? But you go up to the toll booth and describe your keys. Tell them I sent you."

"Oh, thank you! Thank you! You must be a
real angel."

"No," he laughed, "but I did just come from
my first experience with an angel. See, just a few
minutes ago I met my new son. You've never seen
a baby boy so beautiful. But I was hurrying back
to work and, can you believe, it was on my way
out I saw these keys lying there! It will forever be
a very special day for all of us. A baby for me, and
lost keys found for you."

The gatekeeper asked us to describe our keys,
and what a smile from him. "Yes," he said, "you
do not know how I thank da Lawd when somebody finds dere keys 'stead of losing dere car. Tell
you what, da Lawd sure with you, ain't He?"

Yes, that's exactly how the man said it. And
exactly how both of us felt.

Now back to the busy, busy hospital. And oh
that awesome milling of people again. "Is everyone on earth at this hospital today? People, people
everywhere! Now how will we ever find where we
should go?"

Another question—*another angel.* With a smile, a lovely senior lady approached us.

"My name is Eunice. I come here for treatment every week. Can I help you?"

Eunice, the senior age smiling angel. "What floor are you going to?"

"We've never been here before. We have not one wee inkling."

"I come here regularly. If you let me see your ticket I may be able to help you," said Eunice.

"My ticket and your ticket are for exactly the same place. The doctor I've been going to for months is in the same office where you need to go."

Unbelievable? Yes! Except that it's all true!

Oh thank you, thank you Lord,
for helping us be odd enough to
recognize your angels (messengers)
everywhere we go.

❖ 30 ❖

WHEN ANNA RUTH PLAYED SOLOMON

Ardmore, Oklahoma, is an unusual town. On their city's downtown walks you can view many names. If you could see this you would say, "These city blocks are built with beautiful red bricks. And look! The names of various citizens are painted on them. What a town! What an idea!"

And leave it to Anna Ruth. She excels in the art of doing things in her own special way. In this case, it's what she calls, "triple love."

One day she tells me she needs to go downtown by herself. And off she goes. For what?

Later she comes back and takes me to town—and there on one of Ardmore's most prominent sidewalks, I read:

WOODROW HULME   CHARLIE SHEDD
    MAYOR   AUTHOR
          ANNA RUTH
She loved and married them *both*.

Odd? But so much fun! And so loving and honoring for everyone! Yes, you can read it on Main Street in Ardmore, Oklahoma.

And that's my lady! Thank You Lord!

✳ PART VII ✳

FORGET NOT THE BIRDS
AND ANIMALS

❋ 31 ❋

WHEN BEANIE CAME TO CHURCH

Beanie was a beautiful Collie dog with an attitude of total love. Big, dark brown, with white shadings in exactly the right places. A pure specimen of her breed and a champion in the show room. She bore first class puppies, and everybody loved them—and Beanie as well.

We had moved to a church in Colorado. A small congregation at first, but not for long. Why? Several reasons, but this one I'm telling you was one hundred percent Beanie.

It was the Sunday before Easter and we had just about a full house. The service was almost over when suddenly "it" happened.

Hear that heavy thud coming down the aisle? You guessed it. Beanie had escaped her pen and of course she knew exactly where the crowd would be.

To this day, some of the congregation will tell you that Beanie said: "Hear I am folks! And doesn't the Good Book say, 'Love one another fervently with a pure heart!' So here I am. My name is Beanie and I have no doubt about two things: You'll love me and I'll love you."

Naturally I put my sermon aside and called to her: "Yes, Beanie, come right up to the pulpit and welcome every worshipper." Which she immediately did.

Beanie gave us a time to laugh, laugh, and laugh some more. To which, I finally said: "Folks, I'll finish the sermon next Sunday. Let's sing the closing hymn and praise the Lord." Which we did.

But praise the Lord for this too. He knows exactly what needs doing in emergencies. And He proved it again. Because following the benediction that Sunday, one of the congregation's jokers rose and pronounced:

"I make a motion, folks. Let's have a rule that nobody ever says, 'Our church is going to the dogs.' No! Ours is the church where the dogs come to us."

Never before or since have I heard a church so full of laughter. And whenever I recall those joyful sounds, I'm just almost sure I hear the voice of our Lord laughing too.

*Praise God from whom
all blessings flow.*

✳ 32 ✳

ARE MULES REALLY WISER
THAN HORSES?

One of my very good friends is Smith Wilson, and the two of us have long been enjoying our mules and horses. Oh how proud we were to watch our mules win our state championship awards on several occasions in different years. We have loved driving our champions up and down our "front" roads. Not to worry. It's quite safe, as our roads are not heavily traveled.

On this particular day we were heading into springtime. Only a few drivers were going by, and they were watching our animals. Now and then a car would stop to share our pride.

Being gentle almost always, both the mules and horses would appear calm and somewhat quiet. But not this time. Even our favorite animals do like to play tricks on us occasionally. And this time both teams were out to have some animal fun. So they said: "Let's take off and make them think we're running away. Rah. Rah. Rah."

First our big white Percherons took off. Down the road and over the hill they went. But oh no! Oh woe! They were much too near the big ditch at their side. And of course disaster happened. Down, down they went; tumbling over each other; and the wagons tumbling over them in a genuine crash. Fortunately there were no broken bones, but oh what kicking they did to get free.

Meanwhile our prize winning mules decided to take off. This too you may not believe. They were off! Then suddenly they stopped short, less than a block away. And I was sure they were having a discussion. Odd? All right, but if you could understand mule conversation you'd have heard something like this:

"Is this really the thing to do? Why should we be running away? This is plain foolishness. All our lives our master has taken good care of us. Consider the many blessings he provides: food, shelter, special care. Let's stop right here and when he arrives we'll apologize. He's forgiven us before. We can count on that again. Hear him saying: 'You are so faithful. I forgive you!' So it's no wonder we love him and he loves us."

Would you believe me if I said...I wonder if the Lord wishes some of us might be as calm and as wise as a mule?

EMORY WATSON:
THE MINIATURE DONKEY GENIUS

How many times did our Lord ride a donkey? Of course, we don't know all such answers. But let's look at a few of them.

He rode on a donkey while he was still in His mother's womb. You remember this story, don't you? This mother and father of the unborn fled to protect their baby-to-be. And then later, after their child was born, these parents had another "Hurry Away" for safety. Yes, run fast again Mother and Father, and hold on tight to Baby Jesus.

But, long after all this, when Jesus was a major adult, there came another beautiful story. He rode in the Triumphal Entry parade on a donkey. "Oh come now," his disciples said: "You're the hero today. You should ride in a man-lifted chariot and we'll be your lifters."

But no, our Lord would ride a very young donkey, a colt never before ridden. So like Jesus, wasn't it?

———❖———

Now why all this about donkeys? There could be several reasons, but this I know for sure. All my life I've loved donkeys. So when the time was right I bought a beautiful pair of young miniature donkeys. We named them Nicodemus, meaning "hope" and Eleandre, meaning "brave". That would be a first class combination for anyone, wouldn't it? And that's exactly what they were.

"First class?" Like what? Like the truth that miniature donkeys are invariably the only farm animals like this: When they come running toward you their first want is, "Pet me. Love me. I want to be your friend before anything else. Yes, even before you give me something to eat, *love me.*"

Do you know any animal of any kind who gives you that message *first* on meeting you? Now that is some kind of special loving attitude, isn't it?

My friend, Emory Watson, who has my first donkeys in his ownership, would say: "Amen. These are first class donkeys with first class attitudes."

Emory lives in Georgia with his wife, Edna, and their two super sons, Tony and Kevin. Tony is a graduate of Georgia University and an expert auctioneer. Kevin is a first class student following his brother's footsteps. Yes, a simply super family all the way. I wish you could meet them.

Up in the northern part of Georgia, there are many folks who love farm life. And often you will find them doing unusual things. Here is Emory building a sturdy little donkey wagon for training our donkeys. Why? Because we want them trained to superb behavior. Our goal is taking old friends, new friends, children, and adults on miniature donkey rides. Why not? These little animals love pulling their pleasure carts. And they seem to get a super gladness out of their training.

In that mountain area almost none of the natives have ever taken a ride with donkeys. But oh, how they love it today. And I wish you could see these two little fellows pulling their customers. Pure love for both donkeys and riders.

After three years, Emory has trained three sets of donkeys. Yes, bringing them to their own expertise and fun. Next year, he will be eligible for retirement and this I predict: Emory will leave his company, but he will keep on training, working with, and loving those adorable miniature donkeys.

✳ 34 ✳

CHUM AND HER BARN SWALLOW BABIES

Have you ever met a mother bird who could make you do exactly what she wanted? I have. It happened just two years ago.

I was outside building a new workshop. Well, "new" is not exactly the word, because we were into some heavy rebuilding. Our base was a little old tin barn from many years ago. It was falling apart, decrepit, and ready to be a throwaway. But that's the kind of thing I like to work on. So I was nearly finished with our rebuilding when we made the "great discovery."

This little mother barn swallow had maneuvered her trim body through a small hole in one back corner of the workshop. And just as we were about to fill that one last "bird door" with cement, we spotted her. She had snuggled down comfortably on the nest she had built on top of a box of nails. She was ready; waiting for her babies.

What could we do? We knew her birdies would be coming anytime now, maybe tomorrow. And they did come very soon. Four of them. And oh how she looked at me. Through her beautiful bird eyes she seemed to be asking, "You wouldn't hurt my babies would you?"

Of course I wouldn't—nor would you. So, considerately, we decided on a "temporary layoff" for our barn construction crew. One or two months. But I told her, "There must be one agreement from you, little Mother Bird. Every day we get to come for a visit. Is that o.k.?" And it was.

Day after day "Chum" flew in and out for baby bird food. Day after day we watched her babies grow. Day after day we waited to finish our shop. Smile? Yes! Work? No, not yet.

Since all this was taking place in the "new-shop-half-done", we naturally became friends. Everyday we'd go to the nail box and get the latest bird news.

Then came the day! The birds' months were up. Mother and babies sat smiling their usual smiles, with that lovely, "Hi Charlie and Anna Ruth. We love you."

So time was up. They had been here two months. And I had seriously delayed some important final moves for my important workshop. "All right now birdies, open your ears. I have a sermon for you: You've enjoyed your 'have fun, eat well, grow strong' deferment. It's been many days for you but zero for me. Don't you think it's about time for you to be on your way out?"

Two of my workmen friends were with me that morning. The three of us had come into the half-done shop together wondering, "When in the world will they leave?"

They stood beside me as I delivered the message, "Your time is up." And I kid you not, those four little birds heard my edict. Looking at me with a genuine smile, off they flew through the little hole. Then, with a final glance at us, they were gone. Gone. Permanently. And oh how I wish you could have heard their mother screaming all day long. "Come here. Go there. Do this. Try that."

Yes, and I really think she was teaching her little singers: "Praise God from whom all blessings flow."

But that's not all. Right outside the main window in our home is an ordinary feeder for birds of every kind. And we were thrilled to see that for several days "Mother Chum" brought her little flock to our window.

Could that be true? Yes, it really happened.

If I were a certain saint from Assisi, this might be a very ordinary story. But I'm not and it's not. Thank you God.

✳ 35 ✳

THE MAN WHO FED THE BIRDS

There were four of them, sitting on the curb, just outside Heaven's main gate—talking about their futures. Three well-known clergymen, and one simple little man not known for anything much.

Of the three clergy, one was a rabbi, one a priest, and one a Presbyterian minister. But why were they sitting on the curb? Yes, they had all died that same day, and they were waiting for Saint Peter to come and check them in.

So at last, here he came.

But Saint Peter had a problem. "I'm sorry. This has been one of the busiest days in history, and there's only one opening left today. So I'll take a report from each of you in to the Lord, and He will decide which of you can come in today. Let's draw straws for who will speak first."

The fortunate priest drew number one. "Well," he began, "I was a monsignor, not an ordinary priest. And I'm proud to say I did so well everyone in our diocese knew I was headed for a choice position with the pope."

Then came the rabbi's turn. "Of all our synagogues," he boasted, "my congregation was known for giving the most money to headquarters."

"Money?" the Presbyterian interrupted. "You

should see the new church *my* congregation built. A sanctuary for three thousand worshippers and a Sunday school building like no one has ever seen before. You just look it up; you'll see."

"Well," said Saint Peter, "as I told you, we're extremely busy right now; but you can count on it—I'll let you know as soon as the Lord makes His choice."

Then, turning to the little man sitting a bit off by himself, Saint Peter asked, "And you, little man, what did you do?"

"Not much compared to these men, Sir. But I did hear there's a waiting room for folks like me."

"Oh yes," Saint Peter answered. "And I'll see that you're all taken care of until the next opening. But dear man, I can't take the Lord a zero report from you. Surely you did some little worthwhile thing in your lifetime. Come now; can't you think of one good report I can take back with me?"

Hesitating, the little man said, "Every year my wife and I fed the birds when they came through, going south. It was so awfully cold. But you see, they came to us because I built some simple little blue birdhouses. Did you know most birds like blue? Each day Mother and I sat by the window watching them come and go. Hundreds of them! And we loved them all. So that's about all I did. But it certainly wasn't anything like what these other men did."

"All right then," Saint Peter concluded, "we have a report from each of you. So you just wait where you are. I'll try not to hold you too long." (Everyone on the Heavenly staff is ultra thoughtful. And so was he.)

The great apostle disappeared through the gate, and everyone on the curb patiently settled in for the wait. Then suddenly, in virtually no time at all, Saint Peter reappeared at the gate and announced in a strong, clear voice: "Let the man who fed the birds come in."

No wonder the Bible tell us:

> *Great is the mystery*
> *Of true godliness.*
> (I Timothy 3:16)

PART VIII

ODD PEOPLE I HAVE KNOWN

36

SAINT EDNA

She was an elderly Chicago lady with very little money. But she was one of those wonderful oldies who said: "I refuse to live each day and not be a blessing for someone." And oh, how she made her goal. Every week she gathered unsold foods and clothing from the merchants in her neighborhood.

Then away she'd go for an area called the "Near Loop." Busy, busy traffic and almost no parking places whatever. Why? Because the early morning shoppers and workers had come and parked there earlier.

In the Near Loop there were many old buildings "in waiting." Waiting to be torn down or for complete repair. Meanwhile the building owners would construct ultra simple temporary shelters to rent to the poor people of the area. Why? Because a little rental income was better than no rental at all.

So once each week, here comes this little old lady with food and clothing for the poor.

Question: Even for her good purposes, how would one little old lady find a parking place so near downtown Chicago?

When you asked her, with a big smile she would give you her secret:

"Every day, all the way downtown I pray:
   'Hail! Saint Edna, full of grace,
   Help me find a parking place.'"

"What? You pray to yourself and get results?"

"Oh my no," she answers. "My mother's name was Edna too, and I just know in heaven she wouldn't be anything else but Saint Edna."

Wouldn't you like your children to think that way of you?

37

THE GULLAHS

Their ancestors were brought to our land as slaves, and they now live along the Georgia-Carolina coasts. Black, black slaves, and terribly abused. All kinds of abuse, including the cruel order: "Never speak your own language again. You learn our English, or else!"

So, the Gullahs learned English as best they could. And if you had the good fortune of making friends with them, you'd be forever rich. For fourteen years, my wife and I lived on the Atlantic coast. Jekyl Island and Fripp Island are great places to get to know the Gullahs. Anyone who has shared the love of these meek people is forever both rich and grateful.

Evalina was one of our favorites. She was a wonderful cook and we loved her invitations to dinner. We could never forget her native food and lingo. She had interesting rituals and fascinating customs; and on our visits she often prayed this goodbye prayer: "May da Lawd work you easy when you gets feeble. And may He send His angels to fetch you when it time you go home—Amen."

Always, without exception, her prayers were like wonderful trips to heaven itself. But she was a joker too. Sometimes we'd say: "Evalina, we've been here so long! You talk like you want us to stay, but sometimes you pray it different. Like it sounds as if you might mean something else." To which she would smile her widest grin and say, "Well, Da Lawd, He talk both way sometimes too. Ain't it?"

Another of our favorite Gullah-talk memories came from John Willie. He was a tall, handsome young man who hired himself out to the hunters. I wonder how many whimsical sayings came from characters like him.

On one particular day John Willie was the hunter scout for a wealthy duck hunter. And on his very first shot the hunter brought down an extra large goose. So off went John Willie in his boots and rubber coat to find the prize.

John Willie was out there for a long time. Then, at last when he returned he was empty handed. No goose.

"Oh no," the duck hunter said, "that's the biggest goose I ever shot. You sure he's not out there somewhere?" To which John Willie called back: "Sir, Ah don't think that duck been thoroughly wounded."

On and on we loved their Gullah lingo. So odd, so very odd, but oh so beautiful. And they were very, very devout, as per this gem from another Gullah friend: "De Lawd, He da gent man know it all of we."

> *See to it that you really do love*
> *each other warmly.*
> 1 Peter 22 (The Living Bible)

❄ 38 ❄

MAY I ASK WHO'S CALLING

This actually happened not too long ago when I was a guest speaker in Abilene, Texas. It was at a beautiful church, and I was leading a three day series. We had concluded our last event, a gathering for senior citizens. And here he came down the aisle, a tall regal-looking elderly gentleman. Age eighty-two, he said. And there by his side was his beautiful wife. She too a senior citizen. Obviously, with her smile she was anticipating what he would be telling me. And so he began:

"Nine years ago, Preacher, my wife died from a long and awful bout with cancer. So I sat there hour after hour, day after day, glumming and glooming. I was scolding the Lord too. I told Him I loved Him, but I let Him know I sure didn't love what He'd done to me. Night after night, same song, next verse, miserable me."

Then he continued: "One evening as I was up to my usual negatives, I suddenly came to myself. I got up from the couch and said out loud, 'This has to stop. I'm hurting no one but myself. I'm living in a miserable world of my own making. Disliking everyone and everything, including myself. Maybe the Lord too.'

"What did I do? I went immediately to the

telephone and dialed a lady I had dated once or twice. Without even saying who I was, I roared into the phone: 'DO YOU WANT TO GET MAR-RIED?'

"To which the sweet little voice answered: 'I most certainly do. May I ask who's calling, please?'"

When I finished laughing, I was about to ask the tall man's little bride, "Were you the one he called?" But then came that certain nudge, straight from heaven. And the directive from there was: "Stop right there, Charlie. It will be more fun if you never know."

✥ PART IX ✥

THE MIND OF CHRIST

MARKEDLY DIFFERENT AND EXTRA ORDINARY, INDEED!

‡ 39 ‡

JESUS WILL RAISE HIS VOICE IF HE MUST

Jesus said, "This is my commandment, that you love one another, as I have loved you." Soothing isn't it? He said the reason He came to earth was that we "might love one another."

How beautiful! But what is this? Today He's in the temple; and whatever is He up to? He's loudly shouting at the merchants: "You are desecrating my Father's house."

Isn't this our peace-loving Jesus who is virtually in a rage? How odd, indeed!

You'd never think that a gentle person with His background and teaching would dare be so brash.

He was born in a lowly stable.

As a boy, He learned the common trade of carpentry.

When he took on the heavenly Father's mission, he chose plain ordinary men for His disciples.

His message to His disciples—and to the crowds—over and over, was "Love one another."

But wait a minute. Who is this in the tabernacle now upsetting the money changer's tables? Hear the owners shouting, calling for help. Yes, but hear Jesus shouting back: "My house shall be called a house of prayer, and you have made it a den of thieves."

Of course anyone with such unwelcome words and actions will pay the price of rejection. And He did pay that price—on a cross between two criminals.

———◆———

But wait again. It's some time later. And who is this knocking at our door now? Yes, my door and your door. Do you hear His voice? Most of the time He speaks softly; but if we're not listening, don't be surprised if he does something really drastic to get us to hear him say, "Behold I stand at the door and knock. If anyone will hear my voice and open the door I *will* come in."

Oh Lord, do I truly want You in my heart forever? Yes Lord, help me to want you every day, all day, and forever.

Sing it with me now,

> *Into my heart, into my heart,*
> *Come into my heart Lord Jesus.*
> *Come in today. Come in to stay.*
> *Come into my heart, Lord Jesus.*

‡ 40 ‡

JESUS, A TIME FOR SILENCE

What grade do you deserve for keeping still when you should?

Jesus had such a superb speaking ability, didn't He? Our Bible tells us clearly that every one loved to hear His words. The men, the women, and oh yes even the little children—they ran to gather around Him for His stories and lessons.

But never forget, sometimes His talk was "zero." Matthew 27:12 gives us this all-time winner. "And when He was accused by the chief priests and elders, He answered nothing."

Thank you Jesus. That's another gem for us: "Silence." And here it is again in Matthew 15:43: "He answered not a word."

What an example He is for us! Let's sing this old time tune together and often:

Lord fill my mouth
with worthwhile stuff,
and nudge me when I've said enough.

‡ 41 ‡

JESUS ALSO QUESTIONED THE FATHER

Of course you've questioned God. And so did Jesus.

Here He is on the cross. Up to now He's done quite well. No matter the pain, he's able to call down to one of His disciples: "You take care of my mother, won't you? Thank you Brother."

Just then a poor bad man, hanging on another cross beside Him, says to Jesus, "Please, remember me when You come into Your kingdom." And though this criminal, only a few moments earlier, had been mocking our Lord, Jesus, promised: "I solemnly say to you, this very day you will be in paradise with me." Now that's incredible love **plus**, don't you think?

What a man! What a Lord! Yes, Jesus, was our perfect example all the time in every way, even moments later, when He cried out:

My God, my God,
why have you forsaken me?
(Matthew 27:45)

‡ 42 ‡

JESUS, THE GREATEST GIVER

In the last chapter of the Gospel of John, we come to another beautiful love story. This is the account of a real giver. Fact is, this is about history's greatest Giver.

They didn't have the word back then, but the disciples of Jesus were in a deep "depression" two mornings after the Lord was crucified. Peter announced the night before that he was going fishing; and some of the others joined him. They were now still in their boat, as they had fished all night. But the hard fact was they'd caught nothing. The morning came and the weary disciples continued casting their nets. Same result: Zilch.

But look over there! There's a lone figure who just arrived on shore, and he's gathering wood to build a fire. Now he begins cooking, and oh that wonderful aroma of roasting fish.

"Have you any fish?" He calls out to the men in the boat.

"No," they answer. "Not a single one."

So He calls out again: " This time, cast your net on the other side." They do what He says, and are astonished at their nets. They're loaded with fish.

At that, John shouts in a loud voice: "It's the

Lord!"

Immediately, Peter leaps into the lake and be-gins swimming for shore. Then the rest of the dis-ciples come to shore in the boat.

Can you see the bed of burning coals and smell those delicious sizzling fish? Hear that familiar voice: "Bring some of the fish you have now caught."

What would I have said? Honestly, I'm afraid I'd have called out: "Come and see the fish I've cooked for you."

But not Jesus. He lived by a very different kind of thoughtfulness. The kind that says,

Your fish plus my fish
make better fish than my fish alone.

❖ PART X ❖

An Odd Ending

❖ 43 ❖

A FAREWELL MOMENT

Authors love readers who make it all the way through their books.

Thank you! Thank you!

But before we close this down, I'll share this one more thought:

Most of us wait 'til we're in trouble,
And then we pray to God on the double.

Wonder what would happen if each day, we'd ask the Lord: "Anything I can do for *You* today?" I'll bet that would really make Him happy.

Jesus Laughing

ABOUT THE AUTHOR

Dr. Charlie W. Shedd is a master communicator of homespun wisdom. He has spent a lifetime making God's grandest truth available to the simplest of folks.

Dr. Shedd served as a Presbyterian minister for over 50 years. He was the shepherd of small country churches and big city cathedrals. Along the way he walked beside janitors, farmers, physicians, and presidential cabinet members. "Pastor Shedd" never met a stranger, or left anyone who did not feel richer for being in his presence.

He has authored 40 books, written nationally syndicated columns, and been a favorite guest of numerous television and radio personalities. He is credited with being the originator of the Christian weight-loss movement, and along with Bill Cosby, he helped plant Quest courses in thousands of middle and high schools across the country.

Perhaps more than anything, save his role as a husband and father, Charlie will be remembered for advice on love and relationships. The high-water marks for these efforts can be found in the classic books, *Letters to Karen* and *Letters to Philip*, which have sold in the millions. He mentored three generations in the art of keeping Christ and joy in the heart of relationships.

Charlie Shedd has come to personify the best ideals of Christian counseling. He knows the pain life can bring. He knows how to communicate God's love and wisdom directly to aching hearts.

Learn more about Dr. Shedd and his books at:

www.CharlieShedd.com

or

1-800-777-7949

or

Balcony Publishing, Inc
P. O. Box 92
Salado, TX 76571